Introduction

I0470561

Defining how and why many CEOs and business owners have such troubles getting people to accomplish their most important jobs and tasks while remaining engaged within the organization is a constant struggle. Based on my experiences in various organizations, I will offer insight which will give leaders solutions to engage their employees resulting in higher accomplishments for everyone.

I have moved my way through organizations in my career and have noticed a major flaw exists within many organizations: A business plan exists but no business model. I delved into my theory deeper and realized when it came to teaching leadership courses or supervisory training programs, many of those programs did not teach toward a business plan or business model. That left one question remaining: Were the leadership methods being taught helping or hindering the organization?

The primary problem most companies face is they do not understand nor do they have key performance measures incorporated into every department of the organization. In today's workplace most employees do not know if they are winning or losing in their job. Creating a business model that supports your organization and every manager or leader within it is the start. You may be thinking you have great personnel in these positions already, and I agree. However, if you want to improve and have true Key Performance Indicators (KPIs), you need to have performance measures before you have KPIs. After that you must understand and offer the tools necessary to track performance measures and provide the means to engage *every* employee within the organization.

Why

It is not uncommon for someone to ask me why I started doing this type of work, or why I am so passionate about teaching. I can honestly say I am the most unlikely person to be in the position I am now. It was not a direction I thought I would go in life. People often say we create our own destiny; that is what I did. This does not mean the road was not bumpy. There were plenty of jostles to get me moving in the right direction.

Growing up in a Midwestern family described as "normal" was pretty decent. I have a twin sister and an older brother. My brother was an All-American Athlete and remains one of the most intelligent people I know. My twin sister was a model student and had excellent grades. Then there was me.

Every high schooler has that moment where they sit down with their guidance counselor and are asked that dreaded question: "What do you want to be when you grow up?" This ritual took place in alphabetical order meaning my sister went right before me. I will never forget her smiling, happy face when she left the office with a list of careers and colleges in hand. Then it was my turn. I walked in and saw the counselor had nothing on her desk. Where was my paperwork showing I had a bright future? She looked at me and said, "Matt, I don't know how to tell you this, but I really don't think you are smart enough for college." I was stunned. No, I was not an All-American or a 4.0 GPA student, but was it that bad? The counselor reached into her desk and pulled out several tri-fold brochures for the military and one for a trade school. I was bid adieu and sent on my way.

I was seventeen and I was devastated. I thought, *"What is the point of continuing with school if I am destined for nothing?"* I became the most miserable person to be around. After about thirty days my dad sat me down and asked what was wrong. It was clearly more

        © A s c e n d   B u s i n e s s   S t r a t e g i e s

than a teenage funk. I told him the story and he looked at me thoughtfully. He was a man of few words, but when he spoke, his words had meaning. He sat on the edge of his chair and said, "The way I see it, you have two options: You can either take what she says and believe it, or you can prove her wrong." He then walked out of the room. We did not talk about that conversation for the next fifteen years. Today I have a seventeen-year-old daughter and can only imagine how he felt that day.

The easiest way to not stay living at home as you become an adult is to go to college. I focused on finding a college and was accepted. However, after two years I was informed I was not meeting the minimum academic requirements. I was given one more semester to shape up. It was at this point I knew I needed to do something differently. I realized I had never been taught how to learn. My brother and sister learned by reading a chapter, taking some notes, and remembering all the details. That method did not work for me.

My learning method became a commitment to going to class and learning the materials so well I could teach them to someone else. It worked out great for my fraternity brothers because they were no longer forced to go to class. They knew I could teach them what they needed to know later that day. Do I recommend that? No. That is the way it was then.

Well, after college comes life: I got married, had two children, and a good job – a dependable job. One day someone in my organization came up to me and said, "You know, if you went back to school and got your MBA, we would fast track you into a management position." Can you imagine what went through my mind? *"Hell no! I am not going back to school, especially graduate school."* I did not think I was smart enough but found myself enrolled in graduate school anyway. I ended up getting a 4.0 and my MBA.

My graduation was on a Friday, and I remember it well. My dad came up to me after the ceremony and told me he was so proud of me. Remember: He was a man of few words so that meant a lot. Then he mentioned how he remembered the conversation we had so long ago. Being reminded of my high school guidance counselor annoyed me a bit, I admit. I said, "I'd like to take my MBA diploma and 4.0 and go stick it up her butt." Then he told me that she had passed away, but he had made sure no one told me. Dad wanted me to see I had not achieved my goal to throw it into her face but rather did it for myself.

Importance

Shortly after graduating I began teaching for a university and have been teaching for over thirteen years. After nearly eight years of teaching, I realized students wanted more than just theory. They wanted to be taught what they needed to do to be successful in leadership. I had studied and trained in some of the best programs around. None of them were offering tools to show you how to lead and manage.

A few years later I was asked to develop my own company and create my own materials with a partner, but I was the one running things. You can only imagine what went through my mind. Thoughts about competing with some of the best known leaders in the world scared me – A Lot. I knew if I was going to enter into that arena, I had to outwork them. So I did.

In order to develop a business, I needed to do what I taught. First, I wrote a business plan. Next, I developed an organizational chart. Then, I figured out financing and a business model for revenue. I kept going with the tasks at hand, knowing exactly what I needed to bring in each month to meet my goals and put in my time, as they say. My mentor kept pushing me by saying, "That's great, but I know you can do more."

Stop! I was pushing myself so hard and fast I was making mistakes. I needed to find ways to have other people duplicate what I was doing so I did not kill myself – literally.

I started finding people who were living the lifestyle I wanted and dreamt about. I was working my ass off but was not getting to that point. What next? I dove in and figured out something was missing. While interviewing, I asked one of the people I was researching how he was able to travel and do the things he wanted to do. He answered, "I designed my life to be this way." That sentence was short and precise – golden to me – and I realized I was missing the most important piece of the business puzzle. He showed me how his system worked which included total accountability for all of his employees. It did not matter if he was in Europe, California, or his favorite place, Las Vegas, he could monitor his team's performance to see if they were hitting their marks.

I immediately asked myself a very important question: What is the overall goal of management? The answer puzzled me. Right away I created a goal: The goal of management is to create an environment in which people will work together to achieve a common goal while feeling valued in the process.

I then decided to figure out what a healthy organization must have in order to meet that definition. To achieve a healthy, productive, and happy workplace you must

> Provide clear goals.
> Provide adequate feedback.
> Provide a balance of skills *vs* abilities.
> Make employees feel connected.
> Never devalue an employee's time.

Knowing what was necessary for a healthy organization gave me a quest. I could make the optimal conditions a reality by teaching them to everyone who wanted to learn them.

Matthew J Cowell, MBA

 ©Ascend Business Strategies

High Achievers
Leadership Training

Company Name: _____ Date: _____

Please rank each statement below on a scale of 1 to 5 with 1 as the weakest and 5 as the strongest.

Energy	1	2	3	4	5
1. We have a clear mission in writing that has been properly communicated and is shared by everyone.					
2. Everyone has goals and is focused on them.					
3. Everyone is engaged in regular weekly meetings and we review progress.					
4. We have a current method of measuring our progress that is easily available to everyone.					
5. Our yearly goals are clear and have been communicated to everyone.					
Total					

Connections	1	2	3	4	5
1. Our purpose is clear, and we are hiring, reviewing, rewarding and firing around our purpose.					
2. Our core business is clear and our systems and processes reflect that.					
3. My immediate Supervisor is the right person for the job.					
4. The people I supervise are the right people for the job.					
5. Those I supervise are open, honest and demonstrate a high level of trust.					
Total					

© A s c e n d B u s i n e s s S t r a t e g i e s

Influence	1	2	3	4	5
1. My immediate Supervisor is empowering and leads with the best interests of the organization in mind.					
2. Those that I supervise perform their day-to-day activities with the best interests of the organization in mind.					
3. Our accountability chart (organizational chart of roles and responsibilities) is clear and complete.					
4. My immediate Supervisor is open, honest and demonstrates a high level of trust.					
5. All teams clearly identify, discuss, and solve key issues for the greater good and long term progress.					
Total					

Integration	1	2	3	4	5
1. We have a budget and are monitoring per business unit, and the Leader has control.					
2. There is a system in place for receiving regular employee feedback, and issues are addressed in an appropriate amount of time.					
3. Our systems and processes are documented, simplified, and followed by all.					
4. All meetings have a printed agenda, a clear start and end time as well as a clearly defined purpose.					
5. We have a proven process for doing business with our clients. It has been named and visually illustrated, and everyone is adhering to it.					
Total					

Score Results	1	2	3	4	5
Total number of each from the sub-groups					
Multiply each by	X1	X2	X3	X4	X5
Total for each column					
Add all five numbers to determine the percentage score that reflects the current state of your Company.					

If your score falls between

100% - 91:   High Performance

90% - 80:   Innovation

79% - 65:   Engagement

64% - 50:   Courage

49% - 35:   Frustration

34% - 21:   Worry

20% - Below: Apathy

Filling out the Business Analysis at least twice per year will clarify all gaps, put those issues into action, and ultimately enable you to continue to climb toward 100%. The goal is progress, not perfection. You might feel frustrated that your score is not as high as you would like it to be. Yet success is not based on where you are but on how far you have come. If you were at 55% last year and 63% this year, that is success. The next year you may reach 72%, and if you are committed, that percentage will keep climbing higher.

High Achievers
Leadership Training

7
High Performance
(Love, Harmony)
100-91

Works from a true understanding that what is within creates what is outside. Focuses on creating a positive experience for all. Sees the gift and possibility in anything. The realm of "magical coincidence."

6
Innovation
(Objectivity, Openness)
90-80

Sets aside ego, personal agendas, and perceived restrictions. Explores possibilities from all angles. Quests for, seeks, and focuses on the most effective solution to the problem or goal.

5
Engagement
(Motivation, Tolerance)
79-65

Desires to bring value and be a contributor. Has basic enjoyment of the enterprise. Focuses on assets and strengths rather than limitations and detriments.

4
Courage
(Bravery, Resolution)
64-50

Trusts in the possibility of a positive future (despite evidence that a positive future is not likely or predictable).

3
Frustration
(Anger, Egotism)
49-35

Focuses on fighting and jockeying for position against (not with) others. Feels that the external world (both people and circumstances) must be resisted.

2
Worry
(Anxiety, Craving)
34-21

Believes that one must protect against almost certain loss, attack or disappointment.

1
Apathy
(Shame, Dispiritedness)
20-▼

Fundamentally unable to see or work towards a positive work culture.

Copyright High Achievers Leadership Coaching 2014. This document may not be reproduced in any form without written consent from High Achievers Leadership Coaching. highachieversleadershipcoaching.com

The 7 Levels of Engagement

Level 1 - Apathy

Prevalent emotions:

- Sad
- Anger
- Fear

Is cortisol being released?

Yes, the three emotions mentioned above activate cortisol and have the adrenal glands produce large amounts of cortisol in the body.

Mental Response

People are withdrawn or shut down – fight-or-flight response. Depression is common in this level because their emotions are overwhelming, and they cannot cope with them.

Organizational Impact

When an organization is at this level, they often seek "miraculous" help, but changing these behaviors is extremely difficult. What they should do is begin finding clarity by linking strategic objectives around what and where the organization is going. Try to eliminate or remove any saboteurs from within the organization.

Stepping out of this level

When working with someone or an organization that is at this first level of effectiveness, clear boundaries and expectations are needed. If you are supervising someone at this level or in a workplace relationship, tight accountability is key. It is normal for people to need a specific plan with consequences spelled out to move them out of this level.

 © A s c e n d   B u s i n e s s   S t r a t e g i e s

Level 2 - Worry

Prevalent emotions:

- Sad
- Anger
- Fear

Is cortisol being released?

Yes

Mental Response

It is difficult for people to connect with their body at this level. With their chronic and ongoing life, worry often manifests as a general feeling of unease. This level has heightened amounts of adrenaline and cortisol, and the body is more prone to cancer.

Organizational Impact

When one is operating at this level, he/she will often look for some sort of intervention that promises control and certainty, but what is much more effective is a clear-headed and innovative look at opportunities and threats. It is vitally important that fears are talked about, taken seriously and truly heard by leadership.

Stepping out of this level

In the stage of worry, people tend to refuse to stand up for themselves. This is a level of frenzy and paralysis. Often the most helpful intervention is to help move someone into focused, positive action. If you are supervising someone at this level, rationality and action are key. Worry tends to make things look bigger and more problematic than they actually are. The effective manager will acknowledge the worry with compassion before helping the person make an accurate assessment and action plan.

 © A s c e n d   B u s i n e s s   S t r a t e g i e s

Level 3 - Frustration

Prevalent emotions:

- Anger   • Fear

Is cortisol being released?

Yes

Mental Response

People at this level are very competitive and combative. The adrenaline rush of anger manifests as heat, ready to boil over at any time. When an organization is at this level, there is a tremendous amount of internal competition. People feel a strong need to get "credit" for their accomplishments, and sometimes will even take the credit for others' accomplishments if they feel it will help them get ahead.

Organizational Impact

This level needs a positive leader who is more focused on collaboration than competition. Efforts must be made to build (or restore) trust slowly. The frustration level very quickly looks for things to criticize and reasons to stay separate and prove superiority. The organization should invest in a program that aligns goals, values and vision. Helping the team develop action plans to pull them through can be very impactful.

Stepping out of this level

In the level of frustration, what keeps people from moving to a higher level is their refusal to be open to the possibility they are not right, or even if they are, their commitment to their own position at all costs is not effective. If you are working with this person, he/she needs to be called to be his/her best. Challenging him/her to be bigger than the issues, focusing on productive strategies and aligning visions are all effective interventions.

 © A s c e n d   B u s i n e s s   S t r a t e g i e s

Level 4 - Courage

Prevalent emotion:

- Fear

Is cortisol being released?

Yes

Mental Response

At this level there is a new sensation of "heart-felt" feelings. This is where the heart physically feels as if it is opening and becoming softer, even bigger. This level brings exploration, accomplishment, fortitude, and determination. People at this level are generally not interested in conflict, competition or guilt, and thus they feel safe to be around.

Organizational Impact

At this level people are willing to take a chance by giving things a try. In order to keep organizations going in this level, every small victory and accomplishment should be celebrated. People need to know their courageous acts are what is sought and appreciated. For a leader this is not about controlling things but rather providing very close and intentional support to the group or organization.

Stepping out of this level

In the level of courage, what keeps people from moving to a higher level is the refusal to get up one more time and try again. Courage needs acknowledgement of progress so the person/organization has motivation to stay the course. Look at what he/she has accomplished and see how far he/she has come. Remind him/her baby steps are needed, and it is important to monitor progress.

Level 5 - Engagement

Prevalent emotion:

- Happy

Is cortisol being released?

No

Mental Response

At this level the distinction between fears and excitement becomes apparent, and people are aware that "butterflies in the stomach" can have multiple interpretations - restricting or enlivening. Engagement feels productive, fun and is a solidly satisfying level. It is, however, only midway through the higher levels, and there are still opportunities for lower-level energies to intrude. People can become irritated, afraid, and even hopeless from time to time.

Organizational Impact

When an organization is truly in Engagement, so much is possible. Meetings are productive, people help each other, and there is a sense of participation. To move the organization or group to an even higher level takes bold, courageous levels of leadership focusing on vision and organizational goals.

Stepping out of this level

In the level of Engagement, what will keep people from stepping up to a higher level is the refusal to set aside their own egos for the sake of something bigger than themselves. Extended DISC can help explain motivators and how they react in pressure situations. People in this level will be eager to learn, grow and develop. They will learn from feedback and ultimately listen to you and learn from you.

 ©Ascend Business Strategies

It is imperative that you not focus on negative things. The only thing that drives them is positive influences and the desire to improve.

 © A s c e n d   B u s i n e s s   S t r a t e g i e s

Level 6 - Innovation

Prevalent emotion:

* Happy

Is cortisol being released?

No

Mental Response

At this level people are becoming more conscious of the fact their body sensations are not good or bad but are simply information. Ability to confront difficult things from a physiologically calm, centered place is possible.

Organizational Impact

People hold themselves co-responsible for the success of the venture, so top-down management is not needed and will feel as though it is holding you back. Work with or in an organization, truly in the level of innovation, is a dream come true. Expansion and high-level collaboration are themes. There is no problem an organization in Innovation cannot solve. Organizations in Innovation look nothing like traditional organizations.

Stepping out of this level

The level of Innovation is a powerful force. Here you want to share research-based information (brain, consciousness) and refrain from calling forth tight accountability. If a person is truly in this level, he/she does not need it. What he/she needs instead is space to explore and expand. People in Innovation are likely to rebel against any kind of micromanagement. They do not need it, and it does not interest them.

Level 7 - High Performance

Prevalent emotion:

- Happy

Is cortisol being released?

No

Mental Response

At this level people feel their bodies all the time and are exquisitely aware of any changes in their body or surroundings. Thus they are grounded and have the ability to ground and heal others. At this level there is a sense of gratitude and appreciation. The capacity for deep intimacy and devotion is possible; there is a purity of motivation. Here you find an ability to trust one's intuition, unconditional acceptance, serenity, completeness, healing, and profound patience.

Organizational Impact

Organizations or groups at this level are very rare. The world we live in is not constructed for this. In true High Performance rules, contracts, and written agreements are not needed as they are in the lower levels of organizational engagement. However, sometimes we experience group moments at this level, and they feel amazing, fulfilling and even miraculous. There is an experience of joy knowing nothing external is needed. Groups get things done out of passion.

<u>Stepping out of this level</u>

At this level all that is needed is to keep expanding the capacity for love as a commitment to choosing, staying and receiving. The field of High Performance is a culmination of love, trust, integrity, and creation.

By understanding the levels of engagement, organizations need to determine where individuals, groups and the organization are as a whole. Managers need to focus on what they can do to step up a level or two. Each step in level will bring drastic results to each organization. It takes time, patience and practice to move up a level, but in order to see change, the discipline to perform these steps must be developed.

The High Achievers Framework

As I started to research the overall concepts of leadership, I realized one common thing – consistent behaviors over time. Why do people not perform consistently over time? I was really intrigued with the psychology of this topic.

While doing my research, I came across a book which explained if you focus on certain things, you can release the four happy chemicals of the brain. Then it hit me, and I was happy. My framework would be centered around making people happy. That is what the High Achievers Framework is designed around – releasing the chemicals in the brain that make people happy.

The High Performance Business Model

I realize we teach people how to write business plans and read financials, but we do not effectively teach companies how to operate with accountability within their organization. Then it dawned on me: We did not have to do that in the past. Today people want to know if they are hitting the marks. They want to know if they are doing a good job. They want immediate feedback.

This model has been designed to ensure that it was built around the happy chemicals of the brain:

- Dopamine
- Oxytocin
- Serotonin
- Endorphins

I go into the various impacts of these chemicals in our workshops. You just need to know that by doing certain activities and structuring an organization around them, you can create a happy workplace with happy employees.

Organizational Purpose

Purpose is arguably the reason for existence, and the same holds true for the organization you own or for whom you work. What was the drive, motive, or reason the founders of your organization wanted to help, support, or provide for others?

This is often overlooked and forgotten as companies grow and season because the message is seldom passed down from one generation to the next. Employees need to know the purpose which is really the mission. Why do you exist and what can you do to help keep that purpose alive?

Most businesses have a fundamental story that exists. The reason varies from owner to owner, depending on what their initial goal was. Perhaps they needed to develop a better X or find a way to provide for their family and were good at doing something. The story has value and the message needs to get out. Instilling the message to every employee helps he/she see why the values and purpose are important.

Products/Service

It is no secret you must define what your product or service is, and why you exist as an organization. Once you know that, you need to refine it. Yes – refine it. Then keep refining it until you can tell, beyond a reasonable doubt, who your target market is and why you need help in this area.

Apple is one of the few companies that can create a product and market it without truly knowing who its customers are. Yes, you may have the best product in the world, but if your marketing is not as good as Apple's, you need to refine it. Here are a few tips:

- Tell your story.
- Allow people to see the real you.
- Connect your story to how you can help them.
- Show them how you can help.
- Give them a call to action.

Customers

Once you have identified the target market and identified the customers, find a way to reach them. I am amazed at how easy it is to reach large numbers of people without even having a full sales team. You still need sales people, but if you use technology, you can cut your sales team in one-half. How? Use the Internet. Go out and find the best Internet marketing person you know and hire him/her. He/she will not be cheap, but he/she will do something you cannot. In the world of the Internet, you are not a sales person because you are a teacher. You must be able to teach and inform without selling. This sounds crazy, but that is the culture of today's world. You have to recognize people learn, shop, and then purchase. The only way you are going to get that initial reach is to educate them. This is truly important, and if you have competitors that are stuck in the old sales mentality, you will have a competitive advantage if you embrace the Internet and its value to your target client base.

Taking this approach does not mean you get your website ranked. Your focus is on getting your teaching pages ranked and then directing people back to your website to learn further detailed information. Furthermore, you want to use video on your website to help connect with potential clients and make your organization memorable. If you do not do this, you are really behind the curve.

Defined Processes

Defined processes are a lackluster subject to many people making them want to skip over this section. However, *Do Not Do It*. Defined processes are defined as the following: how you make money, your standard operating procedures, your personnel policy manuals, and how you do business. In short, it is your business plan. How do you plan to operate? What are your mission, vision and values within your organization? It may involve transferring inventory from one area to another, or how you want someone to complete a transaction on your Point of Sales system. Too many people stop here in their plans, hiring supervisors to implement everything and complete the task.

I was recently working with an extremely profitable, large pharmaceutical company. They are big players in the industry, but they could not tell me how much they made from each project. I kept explaining they needed to define their processes and develop strategies to determine how many studies, research and development, and other things cost in comparison to the return. They said it would be a huge task to track all that data and were not sure it would make a difference. Yet, they kept saying they wanted to improve efficiencies as one of their strategic objectives and we were going to try to measure it. I struggled with this.

It was not until I was sitting with one of their head researchers that I realized they did not have real performance measures within their company. The CEO of this company kept telling me he had some of the most intelligent people in the world working for him with many of his staff members having PhDs or multiple degrees. Based on that information I took it for granted that everyone understood the difference between key strategic objectives, and performance measures. I was wrong.

After explaining to them they had defined processes, not performance measures, we were able to get the project back on track quickly. Awareness and understanding is a key component to organizational efficiency.

Defined Values

This level of the High Performance Business Model is my personal favorite. In today's world we are way over-stimulated. Our brains can only absorb so many bits of information in a day. We also know the human brain receives messages in a very distinct way. The messages come in; then the limbic part of the brain has to send neurons to the prefrontal cortex where those neurons relate to similar experiences from the past. We try to overdue what the brain can absorb. When we multitask, we actually drop our IQ. It can lower thirteen points just by trying to do too much. I do not know about you, but I do not have thirteen points I can surrender.

One company value I work closely with is *Be Present*. You need to stay in the moment and connect with what you are doing or with whom you are talking. Due to overstimulation our brains are working on overdrive, making staying present very difficult for most people. Our brains just start to wander, and as a result, it takes us awhile to recapture the present. It is a learned skill which needs to be given more emphasis. Being present means your clients feel as though you listen to them, your customers are heard, and most importantly, your employees feel valued. Because there are many things that can be done to stay present (enough for an entire book in itself), we are not going to delve into them deeply in this book.

Understanding your values is so important because it helps create the culture of your organization. Here is something I want you to do for me right now: Stop, and take a moment to look at the values of your organization. Go check the front lobby and see what these values are because they are most likely posted there. Most people do not even realize their organization's values. Someone went through the motions of creating a mission, vision, and values because that is necessary for a business plan. Perhaps it was just lost in the shuffle along the way.

Let me ask you a very important question: Is every employee living those values? My experience tells me no. I have only come across a couple of companies that are truly living their values. It boils down to finding ways to live our values. It does not have to be as complicated as people have made it. What you do is take your values and build them into your performance evaluation system. Find a way to hold everyone (especially managers) accountable for those values. Many people wonder how this can be done and the solution is simple: You should consider adding a section to the performance evaluation system and then placing a yes/no or +/- box next to the

        © A s c e n d   B u s i n e s s   S t r a t e g i e s

values. Some of my more analytical readers are likely wondering why not rate on a scale of 1-4 or 1-5 or something like that. Stop. That is complicated and this is not complicated. People are either living the values or they are not. There is no gray area. Let people know it is an expectation of the organization to live its values.

Transformation will really take place when everyone inside the organization knows they are being held accountable for the values the organization has put in place. The values are the actions or behaviors you expect when nobody is looking. This ultimately is the best way to create a high performing culture. Organizations which truly hold people accountable and measure their values are patient and caring. People want to work for these organizations, and in today's world they are thriving. Believe it or not, people are actually doing more than what is expected. It is all about the culture.

Clearly Defined Accountability

Let me make this clear upfront: I want you to amp up accountability. Everyone wants and needs accountability in order to be successful, but most people think of accountability as micro-management. The difference in the High Performance Business Model is that we are going to drive up accountability by using a process I call Self-reporting Accountability. People who utilize this concept have their employees/team report on the progress (usually) weekly and then have a set time to check up on it. This allows employees to know at any given time if they are winning or losing in the game of work.

When you look at this level in the High Performance Business Model, you can tell it is one of the most important levels, yet it is not taught in any program, school, or college graduate class to the best of my knowledge. People in organizations that know how to do this and make it happen usually rise to the top. Not coincidentally, the organization also rises as a result. What would happen if you had everyone in your organization firing on the most important things?

Imagine what it would do to the bottom line. It would be amazing! However, what is even more important is how employees feel as a result and the levels of engagement you get when you implement a total system of accountability within your organization.

Here is how it comes together and begins to work for you: First, look at any job or category of jobs and determine what the most important elements of that job are. Next, develop a way to track the values so you know if everyone is completing them on time. You might identify that it is important to make a customer contact every week for one of your products. By doing so, you can tell team members you are going to check every Friday at 3:00 P.M. to see if it is complete. How do you do this efficiently? You can have them update a spreadsheet or board as they complete their tasks. Then at 3:00 P.M. on Friday, you go check it. It is a non-negotiable item for you and the employee. I do not care what happens, including all hell breaking loose, you still check this system at 3:00 P.M. on Friday. If you cannot do so reliably, you cannot expect those who report to you to be reliable either. In a perfect world everyone will complete his/her task by 3:00 P.M. on that Friday. When that happens, make sure you congratulate the team member(s). This is essential because we get dopamine releases in two ways: Achieving a clear goal and getting told we did a good job.

I love this example: I was working with the same pharmaceutical company I referenced earlier. They were telling me they had to meet deadlines but were always being delayed due to no one's fault. Hmm…that did not quite add up. I told them to start keeping track of how many delays were due to another department. It was not for casting blame but for figuring out the source of the delay: under-staffed, overly ambitious deadline (goals without any leeway), another project, quality issue, etc. They only needed to record the circumstances for the delay. After several months of documentation, enough data was collected to approach the various departments and explain their #1 reason for delays. This is the moment of awareness.

It is followed by goals. If the average delay was seven days, you start creating goals to reduce it to five the next quarter and keep going until there is no delay. This is total accountability.

Leading without Leading – Influence

Imagine all your employees are hitting their performance marks and are fully engaged in their job. When you design a system that has complete accountability several things happen such as:

- Your job becomes much easier.
- You do not have to continually worry about things.
- You focus on the most important things for your business unit or company.

Almost every time I explain this type of system to someone, his/her initial reaction is that it is micromanagement. It is not. I do not want to be micromanaged, and I know most people do not either. This system is about giving what everybody wants. They want a system that is easy to read - one where they can instantly tell if they are winning or losing. They want to know if they are making a difference. They are engaged.

The largest challenge you will encounter is teaching this system to everyone in your company. It starts at the top. If you are not willing to do this, stop reading this book because the rest of it will not matter. You will not get employees on board if you are not leading by example. Start having accountability meetings instead of staff meetings. Yes, you can update them about projects and status along the way, but it is a frame of mind.

Develop a Plan

If you have committed to creating a High Performance Organization, then it is time to develop a plan for your organization. Decide how you, the manager or owner, will implement the plan first. Master this concept before you present it to the team.

After implementation of the plan is strategized, develop a communication plan. Yes, I mean that – a communication plan. The majority of people will think you are micromanaging them and be on edge as a result. If you know you are giving them what they really want, despite their hesitation, you will be okay. Make it a part of your plan to find positive ways to address those people who do not want to conform. You might hear: I have been here for twelve years, and I have never had to tell someone when I completed *X*. They may be right, but now they do have to and if they do not, they must understand there will be consequences.

To give you a solid start, I have an example of how I incorporated this into our organization. You will have to modify or create something similar. I expect everyone who works for me to cover the exact same things; however, I do not expect them to cover it in the exact same way. They can add their style to it, but they are expected to cover certain materials with a client. The checklist makes it easier to do that.

Learning Has Not Taken Place Until Behaviors Have Changed

Applied knowledge is truly what is significant, particularly in this model. I call the process of creating changed behavior Show, Do, Test. This is broken down into six steps. It is really important you get all of the leaders and managers trained in this process first. Once you get them to clearly understand how this works, then it is time to introduce it to the rest of the organization.

 ©Ascend Business Strategies

Step 1 - Show

As you introduce this to the management team, it is important that you *Show* them some examples of what it is you are going to be doing. Show them examples from this book or download from The High Performance Business Model.

Step 2 - Do

Schedule a 90 minute meeting and explain the following items:

- The High Performance Business Model
- The High Achievers Framework
- The Happy Chemicals
- Timeline for Implementation
- The Accountability Finder

It is imperative you commit to this process. I tell my organizations this process, scoreboard, and tracking is a non-negotiable item. If you do not follow-up on this process – even one time – during the first 90 days, they will notice and assume you do not care. If you do not care, why should they? Stay committed. If you have resistant employees who are busy and make excuses about time, do not accept it. Tell them this is the most important item they have to do, and if they do not get it completed, there will be consequences.

Make sure you let your team know that it is okay to make a mistake during the first run. The most important element right now is ensuring the behaviors of reporting and being held accountable are being formed. Remember: This process is very important and will allow the team to be more linked to the organization, plus they are getting dopamine released every time they update the scoreboard with their accomplishments.

Step 3 - Run a 90 Day Test

Now that you have the managers trained and are holding everyone accountable, allow for some bumps in the road. I have never worked with an organization that has gotten it correct the first time. You will need to fine tune your performance measures, adding some and deleting others. That is acceptable because this is a learning process for everyone.

It is important for you to conduct this for the full 90 days. Some people will try to beat the curve by saying they are better than average because they have figured it out in two-four weeks. That is wrong. You start by taking time to do this correctly so the employees will not view the concept as another passing fad. They are watching you anyway, so why not make sure you can answer their questions?

It is also important to understand there is a natural phenomenon with the human brain. The brain is wired to think in 90 day increments, making it easier to set long term goals with 90 day targets.

Decide if the Targets are Important

You need to set a meeting 30 days from the date you implement this system. This will allow you to discuss as a group if the performance targets are working. Each leader needs to sit down with the key manager to discuss and explain each performance measure. Do not just assume it is working or not working.

Allow for feedback with the performance measures. This is the time you can discuss if certain things need to be changed or modified. Listen to the manager and together decide if it can be changed, but do not allow him/her to use excuses to say he/she cannot complete it. This is the number one thing that will impact your organization.

 © A s c e n d B u s i n e s s S t r a t e g i e s

Monitor progress. I want you to identify if you see a difference in the overall progress of each of the employees who report to you. Monitor the following areas:

- Employee engagement
- Overall happiness
- Amount of times he/she asks you unimportant questions
- Items to make his/her job easier

If you notice you are measuring something that really is not important or is not making an impact in your overall business plan, STOP immediately. The worst thing you can do is track meaningless performance measures. It is very common to track one or two things that seemed like a good idea initially but later discovered it did not make a difference. If that happens, delete that specific performance measure.

Develop an Easy to Use Scoreboard System

The goal of this step is to make a simple and easy-to-use scoreboard to gauge if your team is winning or losing at their performance marks. I have seen many companies think they need to overcomplicate this process, but it is not necessary. The most effective systems are the ones that use a spreadsheet or some type of poster board or whiteboard. Here is why: You need to design a system you can check with ease. If you are working in a manufacturing plant or someplace like that, you want to use a white board or poster board. If you use a computer and want to be the type of manager who can check with ease, then use a document which can connect to the Internet allowing you access from anywhere. This is ideal for organizations with traveling sales forces or multiple locations.

I encourage any manager/leader to think long and hard about this step of the process. The more thought you put into it, the better off you will be. Taking time to do this correctly allows you to be the manager you want to be. I personally want to be able to travel and not be confined to my office every day. Naturally, that meant I had to design a system that allowed me the freedom to check on my team without me having to physically be at the office. So, yes, I designed a system I can log into regardless of where I am, allowing me to visually check the status of all my team. Can you effectively achieve your objective remotely, or do you need a central place for employees to go? I encourage you to think about this from the perspective of the type of management style you dream of having, and then design the system around that. Do not do the easiest method because it is likely not the method which will help you succeed in the long run.

From my experience the best part about performance measures is they provide you with data about companies. I often hear about things being done a certain way because it is best. My response: Prove it to me. It is not that I doubt what they are telling me; it is that I want data to drive the decisions. I want to use the data retrieved to see what is going on within the business unit or team.

The second valuable component of data is it can be used to evaluate delays and frustrations instead of feelings. Remember when I told you the story about the pharmaceutical company director stating that his team always exceeded goals? I then asked him if his employees met every deadline. He answered "No." He thought if his department was doing the best it could, no more was necessary, but an involved organizational structure realizes every department is a reflection of the final result, making every departments' productivity everyone's business. Everyone cares and takes pride. Using data to drive decisions helps eliminate those false accomplishments. It is great his department did not have glitches, but is that really enough?

Step 4 - The Accountability Checkpoint

This is a crucial step for managers. I need you to determine the most effective time for you to check the scoreboard. Once you do that, declare that date and time; cement it in your mind. The optimal time will depend on your business, but weekly seems to be ideal for most business structures. Why weekly? It seemingly provides the best indicators for overall job satisfaction. There are good weeks and bad weeks, making weekly tracking logical. Most people want to know how they are doing. When you can provide them a date and time and hold them to it, you are most likely to get successful results. Then there is the guaranteed once-a-week dopamine factor reiterating what was learned in the High Achievers Framework.

Happy chemical releases of the mind lead to excitement about achieving weekly goals as well as the next aspect of our High Achievers Framework – connections. Immediate feedback on scorecards is positively powerful. The most impactful type of feedback is face-to-face, but that is not always possible if the organization is very large. The next ideal type of feedback is to acknowledge when targets are met and how much you really appreciate him/her as a person. Sincere praise and appreciation goes a long way for the release of dopamine and serotonin. Why not always do that? It absolutely cannot hurt. The important thing to remember is that it is sincere.

Reaching performance targets is ideal, but there are going to be times when a team member does not meet his/her target. You need to ask why and make sure it is a productive conversation with a positive conclusion. I prefer, "What can I do to help you achieve your goal for next week?" I always want the goal to be about us, not just him/her. I want to make sure the team member understands we are working together. However, it is equally important to let him/her know if he/she does not meet the goal the following week, there will be consequences. Some people will challenge this with a brilliant array of excuses to see how far you will go. Do not play favorites or get caught up in their excuses. Trust me when I say everyone is watching, and they want to know what you are going to do. That makes it absolutely important to follow through on your word, even if you are going over to their house for a barbeque that evening. It is that important.

Everyone must know these performance targets are non-negotiable deadlines that must be met. So, when deciding on what performance targets each employee must achieve, you must make sure he/she has complete control over the deadlines. If the employee has to wait on other people over whom he/she does not have control, how can you hold that employee accountable? It is wise to track those measures, but they cannot be a performance target.

Step 5 - Show/Do/Test with Employees

After your 90 day test is complete, you need to get your managers and leadership team trained, monitoring the correct performance targets and making sure each of them fully understands the importance of all the performance targets. They have been and will continue to be held accountable for their performance targets. Then, it is time to share the plan with the entire organization.

Show: Every manager/leader in an organization needs to show what he/she has been doing for the past 90 days. Then he/she needs to train his/her staff about the process. The items to be trained about are in Step 1. The actual training needs to be just as impactful as the training that was done with the senior leadership team. By now the organization is humming, knowing that something is going on. They have seen changes and want to know more. Do not waste your best opportunity to have a captive audience by poorly relaying the message which will ultimately make their jobs more fulfilling and increase their pride in their organization. Explain.

Be prepared for the questions of resistance with thoughtful, insightful answers. They are sure to come, especially from seasoned employees, who are kind of like the older generations who "bah humbug" technology. They will say things such as: "I have been doing this job for nine years and I have not had to report this before. It has worked just fine." or "You just do not trust us to do our jobs." You get the idea. You will likely get some questions or comments for which you are not prepared. Just stay calm, stay the course, and push on.

Explain The High Performance Business Model and share the visualization of its results with everyone, getting them excited or at least neutral. It is like Mikey with the Life cereal: "Try it; you'll like it." As people are positively impacted and departments grow stronger, everyone will begin to realize you are onto something if you stand strong. Remember: You have 90 days experience under your belt to work out the kinks. It is action time.

Do: It is time for you and your team to have your performance target meeting. Sit down with all of your employees and develop your performance targets and scorecards. This must be a joint effort. The manager who tries to do this and then just explains it to everyone will struggle. People want to be part of the solution; this allows them to realize they are a part of something bigger than themselves. This is the integration part of our model, and it is good for endorphins because the closer someone gets to his/her goals, the harder he/she works. That is why setting the weekly performance targets, quarterly goals, and yearly key performance indicators are what drive the winning attitude you strive to achieve.

Test: The next 90 days are a test run for you and your team to get the performance targets correct. Again, do not expect perfection because that will not happen in this stage. You will have to fix a couple of the performance targets as you evaluate the overall system. Remember: If a performance target is not important you should get rid of it immediately. Nothing ruins this type of business model faster than continually tracking something that is not of value.

Step 6 - Start Planning for Key Performance Indicators (KPIs)

The last important aspect of this business model is to set three-year goals and then yearly KPIs. KPIs are those things that keep you going forward. I am amazed how many organizations I work with have goals for the organization but only share them with a few people. If you rely on people in the organization to reach your goals, you need to share these goals with them. If you understand the High Achievers Framework, you will realize when employees are not engaged in the organization, they do not feel connected or energized about it. Sharing goals can change that making for a highly connected and energized environment. Many of the organizations have great managers, leaders, and people making it possible to get serotonin from a good friendship or from peers and a boss they respect. However, they are not getting the complete happiness they could be getting. We all know when you are happy you work harder, you want to work, and you do not complain as much. I really like working with happy people and truly want everyone to experience that joy.

Obtain Peak Results

People naturally like to take shortcuts which means I get plenty of questions about what steps in this process can be eliminated. The answer is very simple: No steps in this process should be eliminated because they are steps toward a better organization. I have spent years working with clients who have a great product or stellar customer service, but their organization is unhealthy. What I mean by unhealthy is they have a sick culture - people are not willing to help each other, lend a helping hand, or make sure everyone

   © A s c e n d   B u s i n e s s   S t r a t e g i e s

succeeds. I want everyone to win, and going through all the steps helps ensure that.

This model is different than Standard Operating Procedures, which does not address how healthy an organization is. If you want your organization to be healthy and grow, you have to implement the High Achievers Framework. It is designed to make sure your employees are happy, and you are reaching complete accountability. After the resistance ends, people may not admit they were wrong, but they will see something dramatic happening – a more functional and operational organization. That is when they start producing more, more profits go to your bottom line, and you are allowed to offer more services, expand, or reward your employees.

The Do's

- If you have 1-3 yearly goals, make sure your performance measures impact those goals.
- Make sure you start with the senior leadership team and run the leadership team for 90 days.
- Refine the scorecards as soon as possible.
- Make sure the CEO/President is 100% committed.
- Explain The High Performance Model to everyone.
- Share the High Achievers Framework and how you are going to make them happy.
- Stop monitoring useless performance targets.
- Get the team involved in the decision of the performance targets by using them to help design or craft your scoreboards.

The Don'ts

- Don't start this model if you are not going to follow it 100%.
- Don't try to shorten the time frames.
- Don't try to do the whole organization at once.

- Don't forget to share the models with all employees.
- Don't skimp on your performance targets.
- Don't just do the scorecards to get them done.

By following these do's and don'ts, you will create a high performance organization. It will not happen overnight, but in approximately a year you will see a major transformation within your organization. You might lose a few employees who do not like to be held accountable or do not like what you are doing, but remember, you are really trying to make your employees more engaged and happier. There is no guarantee you would be keeping them if you did not make attempts to improve the organization.

Conclusion

It is a very interesting time for leaders right now. We are changing and moving so fast that we cannot keep up. Not too long ago I was attending a professional development workshop for the local university where I teach and heard that college students who graduated today will have approximately five-to-seven careers in their lifetime. Three-to-four of these careers do not exist yet. Wow! That is an impact statement. How are we going to prepare our employees for this? How are we going to make sure we have adequately trained employees? It is hard to answer for the future, but you can certainly prepare for some uncertainties today.

Here is an important question I learned from Dan Sullivan, President of Strategic Coach: Is your organization focused on time and efforts or results?

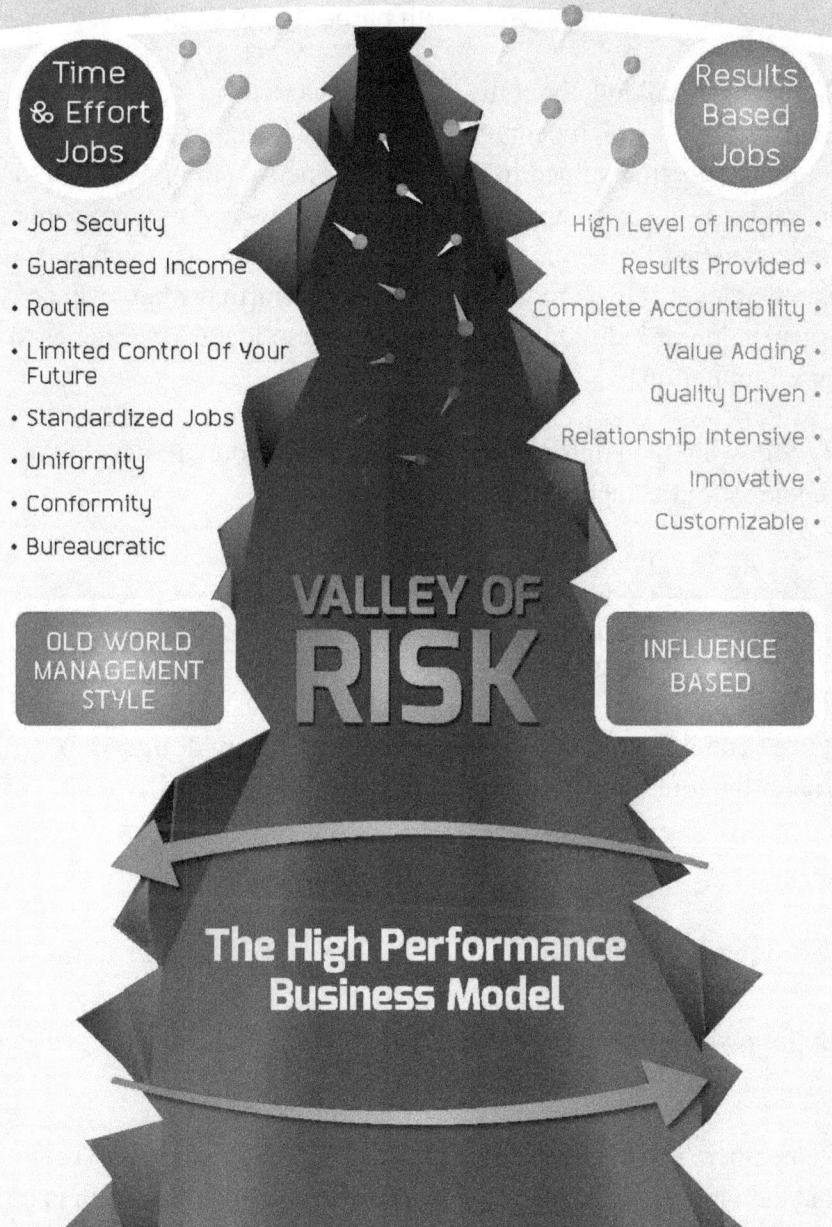

A Results Based Economy

Time & Effort Jobs

- Job Security
- Guaranteed Income
- Routine
- Limited Control Of Your Future
- Standardized Jobs
- Uniformity
- Conformity
- Bureaucratic

Results Based Jobs

- High Level of Income
- Results Provided
- Complete Accountability
- Value Adding
- Quality Driven
- Relationship Intensive
- Innovative
- Customizable

VALLEY OF RISK

OLD WORLD MANAGEMENT STYLE

INFLUENCE BASED

The High Performance Business Model

©Ascend Business Strategies

Teaching people how to utilize The High Performance Business Model is an awesome job. I get to see how people's businesses flourish and grow because we help put all managers and leaders in the mindset to drive for results with purpose and passion.

We begin by talking about the goal of management: To create an environment in which people work together to achieve a common goal while feeling valued in the process. The first thing we need to determine is a way to engage every person at every level in the goal. Understanding the levels is critical; understanding why each person is in that level is even more critical. Once identified what level an organization or individual is, you can begin to identify strategies to raise him/her up.

By following the High Achievers Framework, you will develop people in four categories:

- Energy
- Connection
- Influence
- Integration

It is essential that you realize these four areas were designed to trigger the four happy chemicals in the brain:

- Dopamine
- Oxytocin
- Serotonin
- Endorphins

By following our step-by-step methods, you will be able to focus an organization of complete accountability.

Remember: The change starts at the top with the Executive Team and then moves throughout the organization. When that team is up to speed and has learned from their insights and mistakes, it is time to take the show to the organization's people. Accept mistakes and learn from them. It takes some time, but if you give everything a committed 90 days to work out the kinks, you will find the organization begins to flourish, and more attitudes are working with you than against you. Learning cannot take place until behaviors change.

Creating the scorecard is an exciting and critical part of the process. It should be done as a team effort to include everyone, but as the manager/leader of the initiative, you must insist it is non-negotiable. It may not have been an expectation before, but it is now. Through Show, Do, Test you will make sure you are moving at a good pace, making progress but not being careless.

There has never been a more exciting time for organizations to be innovative in ways to create a new workplace, one that employees have pride in and want to contribute to because it makes them happy. Be the catalyst for more happy people in this world. You will not regret it.

Ascend Business Strategies offers executive coaching and consulting services focusing on employee engagement, personal effectiveness, leadership, and change management. From conflict resolution to goal setting, we not only provide live training but also send our participants home with sustainable models they can use again and again. You will gain competencies through the following course segments:

- Foundation: Your Brain and The Workplace
- Your Hiring Filter™
- The Delegation Navigator™
- My Weekly Planner™
- The Pinnacle Path™ (Problem Solving/Goal Setting)
- The Dimension Model™ (Conflict Resolution)
- Your Meeting Planner™
- Bonus: Your Learning Experience™

If you are not as passionate about your work or home life as you have been in the past, if your energy level and connections are not as vibrant and alive as they have been, if you would like your influence level in your professional and/or personal life to be more lasting and impactful, or maybe you simply want to have greater results from the efforts you put forth on a daily basis, we can help.

©Ascend Business Strategies

For more information:

www.highachieversleadership.com

Whether you are an aspiring leader or want to refine your leadership skills, High Achievers Leadership Training is the course for you. This one-day course covers the imperatives of successful leadership. From planning and hiring to conflict resolution and goal setting, you will walk away with incredible insights and the tools to put these important concepts into practice.

www.successinhiring.com

What keeps successful organizations on top? Surveys show specific hiring practices and tools are directly linked to an organization's success. Effective hiring systems have ranked higher in financial performance, productivity, quality, customer satisfaction, employee satisfaction and retention. We feel success is based on finding the right people for the right job. This course will provide you with the tools you need to have for success in hiring.

www.matthewcowell.com

The High Achievers Framework will help you utilize your wisdom by reflecting on your experiences and the knowledge that helped you get to this point professionally and personally. You will use that experience to create clarity for your business and personal life. You will establish what new habits and disciplines you need to do in order to move forward on your journey. The High Achievers Framework demonstrates how ENERGY + CONNECTIONS + INFLUENCE + INTEGRATION = GREATER RESULTS for your company and your own personal life.

BUSINESS STRATEGIES

To learn more or for a free consultation, contact us

Ascend Business Strategies

www.ascendbusinessstrategies.com

or call 1-866-549-0434

www.ingramcontent.com/pod-product-compliance
Lightning Source LLC
Chambersburg PA
CBHW071543170526
45166CB00004B/1531